Live Assertively Love Your Life

Elizabeth Collins

Copyright Elizabeth Collins 2014

Published by Spangaloo Publishing

Spangaloo Edition

I0436479

http://spangaloo.com

This novel is a work of fiction. Names, characters, events, incidents, and places are the product of the author's imagination. Any resemblance to actual persons, people, or events is purely coincidental

Cover Design: Spangaloo

Ebook Formatting : Spangaloo

http://spangaloo.com

Contents

Forward

When you are able to say no respectfully, you are being assertive. Assertiveness is looking after your own needs and at the same time respecting the needs of others. When you are assertive you can be true to yourself and have good relationships with family, friends, co-workers and bosses. Sounds wonderful, doesn't it? Why is it, then, that we are not assertive on all occasions at all times? Why is it that even when we know some of the skills of being assertive, we cringe when we use them or avoid them altogether?

This book answers those questions. It outlines the steps to being assertive for those of you who are new to this idea and most importantly, it gives you the strategies you need so that you can live a life respecting yourself and others and feeling comfortable about doing so. For those of you who are already familiar with assertiveness why is it that when you're asked to go to a movie you don't want to see, or meet up with friends when you'd rather stay home or go out with someone who no longer interests you, your stomach churns, your palms turn clammy and your heart rate increases? There is a difference between knowing what is right for you and feeling comfortable about taking this step. Throughout this book we'll explore all aspects of assertiveness and how you can use the many skills given in the book to overcome obstacles and feel good about saying no.

When we are not assertive we are being either passive or aggressive. Think of it is a sliding scale going between Passive, Assertive and Aggressive.

We move up and down the scale depending on the people we're with or the situation we're in. We may be passive at work, but not at home. We may be passive with our friends but not with our family. We may be aggressive at work but not at home.

Being Passive

We are being passive, when we place the needs of others above our own needs.

Frank owned and managed a large wheat growing farm in the country like his father and grandfather before him. He was well respected by other farmers in the district and had a good family life. The farm had been built up over many years through hard work, and the only regret in Frank's life was his relationship with his younger brother, Sam. Sam had little interest in the farm and had left a number of years ago to work in the city. He was unable to hold down a steady job and ended up in bad company. Whenever his debts increased, Sam would come back to Frank and beg for money which was always given to him. Frank was assertive in almost every area of his life except when it came to lending Sam money. Although he felt that it was not fair for Sam to ask him for money that he knew from experience would not be repaid, Frank felt guilty about his own good fortune and Sam's miserable life. He behaved passively.

Maria worked in a large department store. She was the assistant buyer in the furniture department, and very capable at her job. Lately, she had begun to feel the pressure of working for a buyer, who was becoming increasingly overbearing and unfair in his allocation of work tasks. One afternoon, after an extremely busy day on the floor, the buyer called Maria into his office and told her that she would need to cancel her holidays. He told her that he had the opportunity to go to an overseas conference and that one of them needed to remain at the store. He had then asked Maria to withdraw her application for leave and grudgingly she did so. Maria responded passively.

On her way home, Maria went shopping at the local supermarket. She was the next person to be served after a lengthy wait in a queue when a woman with three items came up and asked if she could go in front. Maria was exhausted. In refusing Maria said I know you don't have many items, but I'm exhausted and need to go home. In this situation, Maria responded assertively.

Being Aggressive

When we are aggressive, we place our own needs first and do not respect the needs of others. Again, we may be aggressive in some situations but not others. We may be aggressive with some people but not others.

Christine managed a large souvenir shop at a busy international airport. She was continually under pressure from customers and suppliers. Christine had just finished dealing with an irate woman who complained bitterly about the cost of an item she wanted to buy but could not afford when a well-dressed man walked into her shop, accidentally knocking a mug to the ground and breaking it. Christine asked the man to pay for the mug and when he refused she lost her temper yelled at the man and threatened to call the police. Normally, Christine would deal calmly and assertively with an incident like this but as the pressures of this particular day increased, so did her temper and her response was aggressive.

Mario was a man whose life was ruled by aggression. He was domineering in the workplace and at home, always expressing his own opinion and never listening to anybody else. Mario's colleagues were wary of him and even his boss was reluctant to give him any negative feedback. While he was in no danger of losing his job, for he was highly skilled worker, Mario was never offered a promotion. As Mario's children grew older, they became more distant from him, something he regretted. The only people that he treated with any respect were a small group of friends and even they grew tired of his constant complaining.

Being Assertive

Assertiveness improves our Self Respect, Health, Lifestyle and Relationships with ourselves and others.

Assertiveness and Self-Respect

When we have poor self-respect, we don't look after ourselves properly, people treat us badly and we are unhappy. Life can become a vicious circle, where we do little to enhance our well-being and fall into the trap of being a victim. The more we act like a victim, the more we are treated like one.

Feel free to wipe your feet -- I'm a doormat.

A number of years ago, a client of mine had a revelation.

'No wonder my husband walks all over me when he comes home. I lie at the front door waiting for him, just like a doormat.'

When we act in a certain way that doesn't serve us and wonder why people keep treating us badly or taking us for granted, it may be that we are unconsciously sending out the invitation, 'I'm a doormat -- wipe your feet all over me.' Have you ever experienced a time in your life when you said to yourself, 'That's enough. I'm not going to stay back and do the extra work until I get a pay rise' or 'I'm not going to wait by the phone for my friend to ring' or 'I'm not going to let the coach sideline me again. I'm a good player and need more time on the field.'? You change your behaviour and miraculously, other people change theirs.

When the friend rings and you're not waiting by the phone but out having fun, what do you think will happen? It is possible that he or she will go out with someone else. But what do you think they've been doing when they haven't been ringing you? It is more likely that if your friend is really interested in a relationship with you, they'll give you more of their time. Another possibility is finding someone else who will appreciate you and starting a new and more fulfilling relationship. What do you think will happen when the boss asks you to stay back and you say sorry I promised to go out with the family for dinner tonight and then you keep on saying no to unreasonable demands? If you're a valued worker, your chances of negotiating a pay rise or improved working conditions increase dramatically. If your work is not valued and you are treated like a dog's body, isn't it time you looked for work in a place where you were treated well? The same applies to your coach. Every time your coach tells you to sit out you lose the chance to demonstrate just how good you are. If you're not that great at the moment, how are you going to get any better sitting on the sidelines? Tell your coach you'd like to play and if 'No' is the first answer you get, point out how many games you've missed and that it's time to give you a go. You'll no longer be the invisible player.

How do we learn to be a victim? Some people learn quickly, always giving in to others and giving way to feelings of worthlessness. Others learn it over time.

Gina's boyfriend, Troy, was a petty thief and a member of a gang. She had been attracted to him because of his rebellious nature and because he made her feel special. Gina ignored warnings from her family and friends about Troy's bad influence and over time she started to lose her independence and put up with increasingly bad treatment. By the time Gina had come to see me, Troy was in jail, but he still exercised a lot of control over her. She was allowed out of their unit twice a week to do the shopping and had to be by the phone at 3 p.m., in case he rang to check on her. In effect, she was serving her own prison sentence. During our sessions, Gina would reflect on the good life she'd led before she met Troy. She realised that her self-respect had been eaten away, bit by bit and that had come about every time she said 'Yes' to something she didn't want, instead of saying 'No'.

Assertiveness and Health

Good health and self-respect go hand in hand. When you value yourself you are more likely to choose the foods that are good for you, a physical activity that helps you keep fit and a lifestyle that gives you pleasure. Why is this the case? When you place a high value on yourself, you treat yourself well. This doesn't mean that you stick to a rigid diet to maintain your ideal weight or that you make yourself go to the gym three times a week. Food is necessary for our existence and it is meant to be enjoyed. On a daily basis it makes sense to eat the foods that help you feel good rather than eating and feeling uncomfortable or having a pain in the gut. When special events occur it makes sense to enjoy the food that's been prepared and if you're at a friend's place, to honour the effort and care that has gone into preparing the food. If you reach the point of having eaten enough and know that any more will be too much, it is assertive to thank them and refuse the extra helpings.

We have bodies and they need exercise so why not choose an activity you like? If you're stuck in a rut and you're not use to doing anything, check out the things you say to yourself when you see and hear the reminders about chronic illnesses, increasing heart attacks in younger people and so on. Do you say, 'It's all too hard' - the language of a victim, 'I'll start tomorrow' - the language of procrastination, 'There's no activity that I like to do' - the language of pessimism? What would be different in your life if you used the language of assertiveness? 'I don't like going to the gym but I do like swimming. I don't like jogging but I do like dancing. None of the activities offered at this physical fitness centre appeal to me. I'll find out what other options are available.' Self-respect helps us care for our health. Assertiveness lets us choose the options that we enjoy and helps us say 'No' to being a victim, a procrastinator or a pessimist.

Assertiveness and Lifestyle

Do we have to work all the time to get anywhere? Does current technology make us slaves to our jobs? Surprisingly one of the world's leading corporate advice firms has found a way of increasing productivity by getting its workers not to do more but to do less. Management consultants had a reputation for long working hours even before the possibility of working 24/7. The Boston Consulting Group, rather than embracing the 24-hour a day work culture is now encouraging their workers to switch off their smart phones and go home early. They've found that a scheme that started in the Boston head office several years ago giving workers 'predictable time off', initially one night a week has spread to most of the 75 offices around the world and is credited with making workers happier and more productive. Staff can take time for a personal commitment such as getting to a child's school play, having time to exercise several mornings a week before work or whatever was important to the worker. This flexibility led to a culture where it was alright for junior members to leave work at the end of the day before the partners and where workers had a greater sense of being in control of their work rather than being a slave to the corporation.

If you work in place where conditions are pretty good, congratulations! Such places do exist. What if your workplace is unrealistic, demanding and unpleasant to be in or you own or work in a small business where good working conditions seems impossible? Ask yourself this? 'What choices do I have?' You might say to yourself 'I have no choice, I need the money' or 'I have no other options' or 'I have to work like a slave to make my business a success.' Then ask yourself 'How long do I have to work like this? Is this how I want to spend my life? Is this workplace having a positive effect on my health, finances, relationships and overall well-being or is damaging my life?' Making the decision to say no to an unhealthy workplace is a big step. When you make this decision, before you take action you'll need to work out all the smaller steps that will help you move to a different life-style.

Assertiveness and Relationships

When that legendary group, the Beatles brought out a best-selling single, Love, Love me do, they tapped into the psyche of many people who need to be loved. It's easy to give advice to people in abusive relationships and shake your heads in disbelief as women -- and it's usually women -- go back to a relationship where they are verbally and sometimes physically abused. However, if we step into their shoes this is what we may find:

I need to be loved.

I'm worthless, so is this relationship fails there will be nobody to care for me.

With nobody to care for me I'll be alone in the world. I will not survive.

The need to survive is a very strong motivation for staying in a relationship and this becomes more complicated again when children are involved.

What if your situation is not as extreme as this? You may be in a relationship that is not abusive, but not fulfilling either yet you find it difficult to leave and start new one when your underlying beliefs are the same. If you have a strong, almost overpowering need to be loved and wanted then it is very difficult to walk away. But it is not impossible. As you learn to say 'Yes' to yourself and your needs for self respect and fairness and 'No' to the unreasonable demands of others then you can move on to a more fulfilling life.

What are the steps you need to take to feel comfortable about saying no? By using the following approach you'll develop a greater understanding of the power of assertiveness to change your life for the better while improving your relationships and increasing your self respect.

Step One - Place a High Value on Yourself

There was a merchant who travelled far and wide seeking a treasure to delight the emperor. The merchant knew that if he could bring back such a treasure, the emperor would reward him handsomely. His search took him to many countries until one day, while travelling high in the mountains, he came upon an old woman sitting outside a small cave. As he was weary and his day had been long, he called out to the leader of his small group to dismount and prepare lunch. As the food and wine were unpacked, he noticed that the woman had in her hands a bright blue stone that swirled with colours of orange fire.

'What remarkable stone is this? It seems alive!'

'It is,' murmured the old woman

'Tell me about it please and tell me if there are others like it.'

'There are none like it good sir. It was given to me as a gift many years ago by a traveller such as you. He found it in an ancient land and said that it was the last of its kind.'

'I must have it as a gift to the emperor. He would pay well for such a treasure.'

'Alas it is not for sale. It was a gift and as such I cannot accept any money for it.'

'But I must have it. Is there nothing you would accept in return?'

'What do you value most in the world?' asked the old woman eying him shrewdly.

'Why my life of course,' answered the merchant.

'Would you give me your life for this treasure?'

'Of course not!' he exclaimed. 'What would be the point of giving you my life if the wealth that I get from this treasure cannot be used by me?'

'Think on this good sir, as you depart.'

After lunch the merchant left, frustrated at being unable to gain the treasure he desired. 'I could have achieved so much,' he moaned, 'wealth to buy a grand palace and fine horses, gold to entice a noble woman to be my wife, many servants to do my bidding.' Then he stopped and thought, 'This is what my life is worth. It is worth more than a grand palace, fine horses, marriage to a noblewoman and many servants,' and with that he rejoiced for he had discovered his own value.

What value do you place on yourself? Are you important enough to look after yourself and make decisions that enhance your life? I met a woman many years ago who said, 'I left my partner six months ago, when he started yelling at our baby. I realised that if he yelled at a baby he would go on to yell at and mistreat her when she grew into a child. I would not allow him to treat our child badly. Then it came to me and I was shocked, for I let him treat me badly all the time.' When this woman placed a higher value on herself she left the relationship and was happier for it. It is now time for you to take the actions that lead to improving your own self worth.

Action 1 - Clarity

Estimate the value that you currently place on yourself by asking yourself the following questions. Keep a record of your answers so that you can look back on them later and notice the changes that you've made in your life.

Relationships with others

a. Who are the people in my life with whom I spend the most time? List up to 8-10 people.

b. When I am with these people, do they treat me well on most occasions or do some treat me badly?

c. How do I respond to the people who treat me well e.g. what do I say, how do I feel, and what do I think?

d. How do I respond to the people who treat me badly e.g. what do I say, how do I feel, and what do I think?

e. Would I estimate that my sense of self worth in relationships is very high, high, average, low, and very low? If it is less than high, what difference would it make to my life if it improved?

Relationship with myself

a. How often during the day do I use positive rather than negative self talk? Always, most of the time, sometimes, hardly ever.

b. Am I taking steps to overcome any bad habits I might have?

c. Do I look after my physical health by eating well most of the time and doing physical activity?

d. Do I take time for myself to enjoy an activity, a hobby or just to relax?

e. Do I set worthwhile goals for myself?

Action 2 - Choice

Before making any choices it's useful to know something about how to make good choices. While there are many activities we can do and I'll explain one of them to you shortly, before we do anything it's important to leave our choices until our brain is refreshed and working well. 'Doesn't our brain work all the time?' some of you might ask. Yes, and like the rest of the body it can get tired. Let's look at what scientists have found out about the best time to make choices. Whenever you have to pay attention to any task for a period of time and whenever you have to make a lot of decisions no matter how small they are, the part of your brain that is used gets tired. If you're at the end of the day and your brain is tired, it is the worst time to make really important decisions. Deciding whether or not you're going to spend time with someone who treats you badly is a very important decision and needs you to be clear-headed. It's a decision best made in the morning or on a day when you have not spent a lot of time focusing on an activity and making a lot of choices.

For those of you who have people in your life who respect you and who do not accept hurtful behaviour from others, it may be useful for you to read through the exercises to increase your understanding of people you know who are stuck in some damaging relationships. This deeper understanding may help you to talk to them in such a way that you open up the possibility for change.

Now let's look at an activity to help you make important decisions about improving your relationships with others or improving your relationship with yourself. This is something that you can do while on-the-go such as travelling in a train or bus. You will gain even more from the exercise if you can write down or record your answers.

Think about the person who treats you badly sometimes and remember a particular time when that occurred. How do you feel? What did you do?

Now imagine being with this person in a similar situation 6 months from now. How do you feel? What would you do?

Again, imagine being in the same situation 12 months from now. How do you feel? What would you do?

If nothing has happened to change the relationship, then the hurtful behaviour and the feelings that you have will continue. If you never speak up and ask for better treatment, why would it be given to you? If you feel miserable or worthless or resentful when you are treated badly and you do something to relieve this feeling that can be damaging in itself, why would this change? It doesn't always follow that you will choose a behaviour that is damaging, for example, if you're feeling resentful you might go for an energetic walk to clear the tension from your body. Oftentimes, though, when you're feeling miserable, you don't want to do anything energetic because you're already emotionally drained and it's easier to smoke, or overeat or drink. It is possible that the person who treats you badly might change but why would they? If they do, it's also possible they might change for the worse and end up like Troy who mistreated his girlfriend and imprisoned her through remote control.

Fortunately, not all relationships where there is some poor treatment are this harmful and it may be that the bad treatment you receive is more neglect or thoughtlessness with the occasional harmful comment. The same questions still apply, unless you do something to change the relationship, why would any change occur? If the person treating you badly, even if it's only occasionally, does nothing to improve their behaviour, why wouldn't they continue to mistreat you or even treat you more badly over time?

For some of you it may have been uncomfortable realising that there are people in your life who do not treat you as well as you would like. Before we go any further, why not make this commitment to yourself that when you discover the way to stop this poor treatment, you will at least try to make some changes. They might be very small ones to start with and that doesn't matter. Little by little as you start to see the improvement in your life it will be easier to take larger steps.

Action 3 - How to Improve the Relationship through Visualisation

If you have a relationship where you are treated badly and you've chosen a time when your brain was refreshed, considered what will happen if you don't ask to be treated with respect and have made the decision, 'I'll make some changes,' then we'll explore the next step. If you don't have any relationships where you are treated badly, you will learn some strategies for making changes in other areas of your life.

We all understand and make sense of the world in a particular way. For some people, the visual world makes a big impression and it's important to them that their home and their workplace is fairly orderly and attractive. If it isn't, it can be slightly distressing for a disorderly world can create tension. These 'visual' people learn well through images and pictures and store their interpretation of the world within their inner vision. For example, if this person were asked to remember an incident where someone treated them badly, they might visualise the person very close to them, being larger than life and possibly vibrating with highly vivid colours. Try this activity now to see if you absorb information about the world visually.

In a moment, close your eyes, take a deep breath and imagine someone or something in your life about which you have positive feelings. It may be a pet, a family member or friend or even a favourite possession. When you do close your eyes do you see your chosen image even if it is slight blurred? If you are able to visualise, like your environment to be fairly orderly and you find it fairly easy to both recall an image and to visualise even the suggestion 'pink elephant with green spots', it is likely that you make some visual interpretation of the world. Why is this important to know? Because the unpleasant things in your life may be stored in an overpoweringly visual way. When you learn to change these internal images, it is possible to lessen the impact of people in your life who treat you badly.

Annika worked as a dental assistant in a successful dental practice focused on children. She loved her work and had discussed with one of the dentists, the possibility of doing further study and one day becoming a dentist. Her colleagues at work encouraged her for she was very capable and they felt she would do well. Her partner was supportive although concerned about the length of time it would take her to train. Her greatest stumbling block was two of her friends. 'You'll never be able to train as a dentist and have children. Don't you want children? It's abnormal to be in a long term relationship and not have children. Is there something wrong with you and you can't conceive? Is there something wrong with the relationship? Do you really think you're that bright? You were only average at school in science.' And so it went on until Annika started to entertain doubts about her ability to do the study and the interference to her relationship. She longed to say to these two friends, ' I find that when you talk continually about all the things that might stand in my way I start to feel demoralised and I 'd like you to stop. I know you have doubts about my decision but I'm happy with my choices.' Whenever she thought about saying this, Annika started to feel really uncomfortable. What if they took offence and didn't want to be friends anymore? This would create tension in the group.

Annika had read about the power of visualisation so she decided to try it. First she found a quiet spot where she wouldn't be disturbed, and then she saw her two friends sitting opposite her in a coffee shop. They seemed to be very close and very large and their mouths were moving a lot. Annika felt quite uncomfortable. She opened her eyes and took a deep breath. Then she closed her eyes again and rather than seeing her two friends, she created a picture where she saw herself in the coffee shop sitting opposite her friends. She had learned that when you put yourself in the picture, it lessens the emotional impact of the picture. Even seeing herself with her friends made her feel a bit less uncomfortable. Then she decided to shrink her friends. She imagined them getting smaller and smaller until they were really tiny and barely able to reach the table. She made them so small that in the end they had to sit on the table like two tiny dolls. Amazingly, as they started to shrink their mouths moved less and finally closed altogether. The sight of her two tiny friends struck her as very funny and she stated to laugh. Any discomfort she felt had gone completely. Annika kept visualising this image for the next few days before she saw her friends and when they started to be negative she found it surprisingly easy to let them know what she wanted. As

Annika was calm and spoke to them in a friendly manner neither of them took offence and said they were just trying to help her and didn't realise that she was getting upset.

If we can visualise, then we will have some images stored in our visual memory. Here is a reminder of the steps to take to lessen the impact of any of these stored images. When you try this strategy, make the first practices about something that is mildly upsetting until you get use to changing images.

1. Find a quiet place where you won't be disturbed for a few minutes.

2. Think about the situation that you find unpleasant.

3. Notice the size of the image, whether or not you are looking at the image or looking at yourself in the image.

4. Is the image in colour or black and white?

5. Is the image directly in front of you or is it to the side or slightly higher or lower than your field of vision?

6. Is there movement in the image or is it still?

Changing the Image

1. If you are looking directly at the image, place yourself in the image as this will lessen the emotional impact.

2. Move the image to a comfortable distance. You might move it back a little or if it feels better, move it further away, noticing how it gets smaller the further away it moves.

3. If the image is in colour, play with the colour. You might like to change the colours or make them paler even turning them to black and white. If the image is already black and white you might like to add some colour.

4. If the image is not directly in front of you, you might like to move it so that it is in your direct field of vision. If it is already there, try moving it to the side or making it slightly lower or higher.

5. If there is movement in the image, try making it still. If it is still, create some movement.

An Important Note

When you start playing with your internal images, only change them in a way that feels comfortable and right for you. You will notice that as you change one or two parts of the image, many other parts may change automatically. This is perfectly natural as your mind starts to create a different interpretation of the memory.

Action 4 - How to Improve the Relationship through Body Awareness

Not everyone finds it easy or possible to visualise. For those of you who make sense of the world through your gut feelings, it's possible to use these feelings to change your interpretation of the memories that you hold in your body. We'll go through a similar but slightly different exercise to the one using visualisation. First, think about a time when you felt happy. It may be something simple such as playing with a pet, taking a walk through a park or along a beach on a beautiful spring day or being with friends or family members that you care about. Now be aware of the sensations as you remember this pleasant time. Really get in touch with those feelings. Explore them a bit. Where are they in your body? Are they around your chest area, your heart or do you feel them in some other place such as your gut or your legs. It doesn't matter where the feelings are; the most important thing is just to be aware of that place. Now be aware of any movement of these feelings. Are they still or do they shift around and if they do, is it a flowing sensation like water moving along a quiet stream or is it more vibrant, a whirling sensation? If you could touch the feeling, what would it be like? Would it feel soft or firm, smooth or bumpy? Play for a bit with these sensations.

It's useful to practise getting in touch and knowing your bodily sensations through memories of pleasant experiences first before you move onto any memories that make you feel uncomfortable. This is so you can know the places in your body, the types of movement and any other detail about where and how you store pleasant memories. When you tap into the unpleasant experiences, you can change them to make your experience less distressing.

Paulo had just arrived in the city. He'd been travelling for two days, first by car to the bus depot where his friends had said their farewells and once again asked him not to go, then by bus overnight and part of the next day. He was feeling miserable and depressed at leaving his home town and moving to the city with only the promise of a job. Nothing was certain. He found a wash room, freshened up then went to the employment centre where he took a ticket and waited his turn for an interview. His home town had little to offer in the way of work but his friends and family were there. Whenever he thought about them he would get a warm feeling in his chest. The woman who called him into the office looked unfriendly. He handed her his employment forms, told her what he was looking for then was asked to wait outside for half an hour. An hour passed and he still hadn't been called. He remembered what his uncle had said, 'In the city people are busy and many of them will seem unfriendly because they have many problems and lots of stress. If you can be friendly to these people and not get your back up, in the end you'll get what you want.'

Paolo thought about the woman and his stomach went into a knot. He felt tight and hot in his chest. Then he remembered his friends and family and slowly the knots left his stomach and his chest started to relax. He kept thinking about the woman and his loved ones and the more he did so the more relaxed he felt. By this time an hour and a half had passed and he was hungry. He got up, went to the office door and knocked. When the woman called out to come in, he said 'You told me that you would call me in half an hour and as one and a half hours have passed, I wanted to let you know I was still outside.' The woman looked angry so Paolo kept remembering his friends and family so he could stay relaxed. He waited. When it was obvious he was not going to go away the woman said, 'I'm very busy.' Paolo agreed with her. 'Yes, I can see that you are busy and as I've been travelling for two days and need to find a place to stay and something to eat, it's important that I sort out my employment application. Is there anymore information that I can give you so you can finalise my form.' At all times Paolo remained calm and friendly but by simply staying, being polite and asking if there was more he could do, Paolo made it clear that he was not going away. At last the woman pulled out his form, checked it then gave him the address of a place where he *could start as a casual worker the next day. He thanked her for her help and noticed that when he left she was no longer scowling. A job like hers must be pretty stressful he thought to himself and realised he had no unpleasant sensations in his body when he thought about her.*

Action 5 - How to Improve the Relationship Through Self-Talk

The things we tell ourselves can make the difference between happiness and sadness, giving up and deciding to persevere. Professor of Psychology, Martin Seligman, found that if you tell yourself that the problem will always be there, that it will occur in all situations and you're to blame then you'll think like a pessimist. He found that the opposite - telling yourself the problem is temporary, that it will only occur in some situations and that external events are to blame - leads to thinking like an optimist. When you think like an optimist you feel happy and are more likely to have better health and achieve more. This is not to say that it's wise to be optimistic on every occasion at all times for there may be times when it's more useful to do a reality check and consider the negatives, especially if you're investing money. Flexible optimism, that is a positive outlook that gets you through life particularly when there are setbacks and challenges, is a very useful strategy to manage feeling good about being assertive.

Belinda had been seeing Jason for two months. She liked him and hoped that the relationship would continue. One day, when they had gone to the beach for a swim, Jason started to make unkind comments about two women walking along the water's edge. 'Women who look like that shouldn't wear a bikini. You'd think they'd cover up.' Belinda thought the women looked fine. True, they were not trim and toned like a model but what was wrong with that? Then she started to think to herself, 'If he judges these women so harshly, what does he think about the way I look? If we stay together, what will he think of me in ten years time? If he's going to be so judgemental, he'll never change. Perhaps I'm not attractive enough and he's trying to tell me by criticizing other women so he doesn't hurt my feelings.' The thoughts went round and round in Belinda's head.

When Jason suggested another swim, Belinda decided to walk along the beach instead. There was something about walking through the cool water and smelling the salty breeze that seemed to clear her head. She hadn't noticed Jason being critical about other women's appearance before, perhaps it was something about this situation. She knew he'd been under pressure at work so his comments might just be letting off steam. Still she was concerned about the judgement he'd made so she decided to talk to him when he came out of the water.

When you understand the trap of thinking like a pessimist you can take steps to thinking more optimistically. How does this help you to be assertive and enjoy being assertive in a relationship where unpleasant things are said either to you, or as in Belinda's case, about others? The way you talk to yourself will make you either accept the unpleasant side of the relationship leading to feelings of powerlessness and unhappiness or you will believe that you are able to change the relationship by discussing the things that concern you. Optimism can lead to feelings of personal strength and an increasing sense of self worth.

Action 6 - How to Improve the Relationship through Acting

Famous tennis players, soccer stars and swimmers all have something in common with concert pianists, the local basket ball team and cryptic crossword players. They practise. Is it true the more they practise the better they get? Not necessarily. The more they practise the right behaviours whether it's hitting the ball in the centre of the racquet, perfecting a difficult section of a sonata or knowing which clues to focus on in the cryptic crossword, then the better they get. Practising the right behaviour before you go into a challenging situation where you've decided to be assertive increases your chances of managing the situation to your liking.

How do you practise?

1. Decide on the situation that is unfair and what you would like to do about it.

2. If you are able to visualise, even a little, picture the situation with yourself in the picture and change the images as described above in Action 3 - How to Improve the Relationship through Visualisation

3. Be aware of any bodily feelings that you have and make changes to these that help you to feel better about the action you're taking.

4. Work out what you would like to say in the unfair situation.

By now you might be feeling so good that this could be enough. To make sure you succeed take one more step. If you have a trusted friend or family member that you can practise with, ask them to help you. If not, practise in front of the mirror or if you have a camera that you can use to take a short movie of yourself, practise in front of the camera.

5. Imagine you are talking to the person who is unfair to you. Stand straight with your shoulders back in a comfortable position and use eye contact. Now say what you plan to say. Notice if your posture changes as it's possible to slump and hunch your shoulders when you're not feeling confident. Check your eye contact. Be aware of your voice. Did it quaver or was it too soft? Now you know how you come across, keep practising until you're pleased with how you look and what you say.

6. When you've done this, now do all the things that would come across as non-assertive or passive. Again, do it in front of a friend, a mirror or a camera. Let your shoulders slump, lower your eye contact, stand in an awkward position, and speak softly with 'ums' and hesitations. How do you come across? If someone was listening to you and looking at you, what would they be thinking? Now stand up straight, take a deep breath then shake your body. This will help get rid of any uncomfortable feelings related to the exercise.

7. You have an awareness of how you want to come across and you know, don't you, that if you come across passively or even aggressively, you won't feel good about trying to establish a relationship that's fair to you and fair to the other person. So go ahead now, and practise the best way to present yourself. You've already done it, I know, but do it a few more times so that the memory stays in your body.

Relationship to Self

Before exploring the next step, how to place a high value on others, we'll look more deeply at some of the questions about your relationship with yourself. Earlier in the book you did an exercise on clarity in relationship with yourself, the first question being 'How often during the day do I use positive rather than negative self talk?' The more often you speak to yourself positively, the more you will find that your relationship with yourself and with others improves. People who surround themselves with pessimistic people, who go into self-destructive situations and who seek out all that is negative in life find it almost impossible to be positive about themselves and about what life has to offer. Before you take the step of filling your day with positive self-talk, it's important to check out what is in your day. If you are working, is your workplace a good place for you to be? It doesn't matter what type of work you do, it's how you feel about your work and how you are treated in your workplace.

Jose had been working as a paramedic for nearly two years. Friends would ask him how he survived going out to horrendous accidents, seeing people whose arms had been severed, heads bashed in and bodies crushed in trucks and cars. When first he was asked these questions, he'd just say, 'You get used to it,' but over time he started to think about it more. How did he survive? One day after a fatal crash at a railway crossing where a car had ignored the stop signals and tried to beat the train, Jose went to the cafeteria with some of the other paramedics to talk about the day. 'How do you get through the day when you work with these accidents?' he asked the others. 'It's good to talk about it after,' 'I play with the kids when I get home,' 'I like to think I'm doing a good job,' 'If we didn't clean up the mess, who would?' and 'We help people survive,' were some of the answers. Everyone had given Jose the impression that although their work was hard, they had a way of coping and they felt there was some positive purpose in what they did. It was possible for them to use positive self talk as well as other strategies to help them manage what could be very distressing work.

By contrast, Lian worked in a large accounting firm as a trainee accountant. She was constantly under pressure to perform at work and keep good grades at college. It was winter and after several days off with a severe bout of the flu, Lian was called into the senior accountant's office to talk about her absence. This puzzled her as she had already handed in a doctor's certificate. 'We can't have people shirking their work and offloading it onto others,' he explained to her, 'so in future, if you're sick then you'll have to complete your work in your own time.' Lian was seething. She went straight to the Human Resources Department and asked for an interview. Little help was received beyond a few sympathetic nods and the confirmation that this was the firm's 'unwritten expectation'. Lian was stuck. She had taken a traineeship with a firm that promised so much but took far more than it gave.

In this situation it would seem very difficult for Lian to go to work and speak to herself positively. What are her choices? A passive choice might involve speaking to herself in the language of a victim 'I'm stuck here and there's nothing I can do about it. I just have to put up with being treated badly,' leading to feelings of pessimism and hopelessness. If Lian used positive self talk she might say, 'This is a very difficult situation. What are my choices?' These might include reviewing her contract, speaking with other trainee accountants at college and checking out their experiences and looking at options for moving her traineeship to another organisation. If leaving the organisation was not an option and if other trainees were experiencing similar work pressures, Lian could review her long term career as an accountant. Once her traineeship was completed, would her work situation improve or was it a career that she should reconsider? Finally, if she chose to stay in the field, it would be important to set clear goals about how she could manage during her traineeship. These goals would include looking after her health and taking time to enjoy pleasurable activities. Finally, it would be useful for Lian to use self talk that was empowering. 'I've chosen to stay here even though the work situation can be difficult. My traineeship will be finishing in 2 years and then I'll have better working conditions,' rather than 'It's terrible working here and I'm stuck. There's no way out.'

Step Two - Place a high value on others

Assertiveness is respecting others as well as respecting yourself. The skills that have been given to you already will help you treat others fairly. This is most important if you find yourself reacting aggressively in situations where you feel badly used. For those of you who have more difficulty treating yourself fairly, it is important to remember to place a high value but not a higher value on others. There are three actions that will help you keep this balance as you strive towards being more assertive.

Action 1 - Check out your beliefs.

Do you truly believe that it is important to treat others well but not better than yourself or do you have a sabotage voice that whispers in your ear - 'You're not as good as they are' or 'You're far more important than them.' If you do, check it out. Where does this message come from? Has it been with you since childhood? Do you like the message? If you like the message do you like the actions you take because of this message? Sometimes, particularly if someone has treated you badly and you react in a negative way towards them, there can be a feeling of satisfaction - after all they deserved it! Further down the track, does this feeling still feel good or do you regret having had mean thoughts and possibly taking harmful action?

I'll let you in on a secret. All the negative thoughts that you have towards yourself and others have been learned. If you have learned how to be negative then you can learn a more positive approach instead. It has been said that thoughts are energy and when we have negative thoughts we do some harm. It makes sense, doesn't it, that if we start the day believing that we are going to have a bad time and that people will be mean to us or try to rip us off, that we'll have all the posture, language and actions of a victim. If we present ourselves to the world acting like a loser because we believe the world is going to give us a hard time, then it will. On the other hand, if we act as though the world is untrustworthy and you have to get 'them' before they get 'you', the messages that you send out will make people keep their distance or if they're similar to you, there will be numerous clashes and you may not win every one.

Action 2 - Change your negative beliefs.

When you have decided to change any negative beliefs that you have about your relationship with others, there are five steps to take:

1. Write down all the benefits that will occur when you treat others fairly. These can include benefits for yourself and other people.

2. Write down all the negative consequences of treating others unfairly. Again, include the negative consequences for yourself and others.

3. Close your eyes and imagine how you will look, what you will be doing, what you will be saying, how you will be feeling and what others will be saying to you. If you can image what other people are saying about you, what would it be?

4. Open your eyes. Remember, if you find if very difficult to visualise and you're more in touch with the feelings in your body, ask yourself questions such as, 'How do I feel about how I will look?', 'What are some things I might be saying and how do I feel about this?' and so on.

5. Now do the same exercise but this time, imagine how it will be if you continue with any unfair actions. When you have finished, take a deep breath and think of something pleasant and relaxing.

Kylie was determined to change her life. She lived in a small country town and wanted more that anything to live in the city and work for a large organisation that would give her plenty of opportunities. In preparing for the changes she enrolled in computer studies, office management and many other relevant courses. One day her college lecturer said to her, 'Kylie you're very skilled with all office tasks and you're good at speaking out and standing up for yourself. I'm concerned that sometimes you talk over other people when they're trying to voice their opinion. This could make it difficult for you in a new workplace.' Kylie imagined what it would be like if someone kept talking over her and realised that she wouldn't like it. She thought about what would happen if she became more patient and listened to others. Then she decided to write this down. Her next step was to imagine how her new colleagues might react if she didn't change? She thought about this and wrote it down as well to act as a reminder.

Kylie had made up her mind to be more aware and accepting when other people expressed their opinions. This did not mean that she would accept their point of view if it differed from hers, but she would give them the chance to express it. Kylie then imagined herself working in the city. She was friendly and patient with people, saw herself listening to others as well as talking and started to feel warm around her chest. She realised that her body was quite relaxed. Then she imagined herself in the same workplace talking all the time. She pictured others walking away from her and even glimpsed disappointment on some of their faces. Kylie had a hollow feeling in her chest and realised that that her neck and shoulders were tight. Checking in with her internal states allowed Kylie to appreciate the difference that these two approaches could have. She took a deep breath to clear the tension in her body and imagined being on the beach, a place that always helped her to relax.

Action 3 - Practise these changes

When you have made up your mind to change and you've started to explore the impact of these changes, then it's time to practise them. There are 5 steps.

1. Write down goals for the actions that you would like to take.

Goals that are written down and reviewed are more likely to be achieved. Remember to make the goals easy to achieve yet sufficiently rewarding to get you motivated. It's important to write down the date by which you want the goal to be achieved. If you don't write the date including the year, your unconscious will float around quite happily without any clear guidance.

Example: When I am in a group, I listen to people's points of view and I express my point of view easily by 1/8/13.

2. Select one of these goals and plan how you will practise.

While it's necessary to set goals, if you don't have a plan of action you may never achieve your goal.

Example: When I go to the party this Saturday night, I'll speak to a friend. I'll tell them I enjoyed the movie we went to as a group and why I enjoyed it, then I'll ask them what they liked or didn't like about the movie. If they start to speak first, I'll listen to them, and then I'll tell them my point of view. Then I will go up to someone at the party I don't know or don't know well and I'll ask them about their interests. When I've listened to them, I'll tell them the sorts of things I enjoy.

3. Reflect on how you feel about having these conversations.

4. Once you feel comfortable practising this new behaviour and you can do it easily, select another goal and practise. If your first change was with friends, why not make the second one in the workplace or with your family?

Example: I give assertive messages to people who speak rudely to me at work by 12/8/13.

5. Now it's time for your plan of action.

Respecting other people at work can be very difficult at times, particularly when you have challenging co-workers or bosses and certainly when you're dealing with members of the public who can be rude and sometimes abusive. Keeping a sense of self respect and responding respectfully is easier when you:

- take a deep breath to calm yourself

- remember their anger and rudeness is not about you

- let them speak first while keeping eye contact and standing tall

- give clear messages that you have heard their complaint

- only promise what can be delivered.

Tom worked in customer service at the local hardware store. He was responsible for taking orders and refunding returned goods. Most of the customers were good natured but there were always a few difficult people everyday. One day a large man came to the counter and banged a power tool on the desk. 'Broke the first time I used it!' he yelled and started to swear at Tom calling him and every employee in the store incompetent and useless '. . . just like this power tool!' he said finally stopping for breath. Tom was annoyed and took a deep breath. He knew the man was angry about the power tool not working but his language was offending other customers. He stood straight and looked up at the man saying in a firm and strong voice, 'I can understand you're angry about the power tool not working. I can fix the problem but you'll have to stop swearing first because you're upsetting other people - just look at them.' The man looked around and saw the faces on the people near him. He stayed angry and red in the face but stopped swearing. Tom was able to talk to the man calmly but firmly and sort out the problem.

Review

You have travelled the path of learning about
assertiveness and you have been encouraged to
approach the world assertively for your own benefit
and the benefit of others. The many challenges around
assertiveness have been looked at, feelings around
these challenges have been explored and many
strategies have been suggested to make the path
towards assertiveness an easier one to travel. These
strategies have included gaining clarity in relation to
yourself and others; learning the best time to make
choices; improving relationships through using your
inner states of vision and bodily awareness; being
aware of the impact of the things you say to yourself;
understanding the importance of being positive;
practising the skills you have learned and exploring
how to respect both yourself and others.

At this point there is something you need to know. When you decide to live a life in which you respect yourself and others, the challenges will not stop - they will keep on coming. Once you find yourself being more assertive with your family, friends and in the workplace and you feel good about saying 'No,' to people who ask you to do something that does not fit with your values or is not fair, situations will arise where yet another challenge will occur. These situations are necessary for once you master a skill, if you don't keep practising then the skill begins to weaken. 'Why then would I bother learning it at all?' some of you might ask. Because the alternative is for you to be passive and let people walk over you leaving you feeling worthless and resentful or aggressive leaving you with damaging relationships.

When you choose respect and fairness, life becomes more satisfying, happiness increases and relationships improve. It's an approach that serves you well at any age, in any occupation and at any time of your life.

Having chosen this approach, one or two questions might still arise.

'Is it necessary to write down the answers to the questions asked in the book? What if I'm reading on the train or in a bus?'

'Why do I have to measure my current level of self-worth?

The answer to both these questions is similar.

You need to know your starting point to check your gains. Sometimes changes are slow and sometimes they are fast but small. We rarely notice the slow, small changes as our lives are busy BUT if we have written down

'In January this year, I am having problems with my partner/friend bossing me around,' and in June, having practised being assertive you notice that this hardly happens any more, then you know assertiveness is working for you.

Where To From Here?

You have been given the starting points and many skills to help you on your way. A world of change awaits and it cannot be contained in one book. There will be more books available in the future. I always appreciate questions and feedback and if you like the book please go to Amazon and tell others about it via a review.

There will be a workbook available as a companion to this book you can look for it at online retailers everywhere or at Spangaloo

http://spangaloo.com